PRAISE FOR THE INNOVATOR'S HANDBOOK

"Young and emerging designers take note! If you're hungry for creative growth and inspired stories about design innovation, add Hussain's handbook to your growing design library. Hussain's creative prompts and experienced mentorship can propel young design talent to reach dizzying creative heights. This book is infectiously good!"

—PHILIP STANKARD, *ID Lead at 3M Design*

"I've worked with many great artists with beautiful minds. Hussain is one of the finest, and the depth of his creativity is on full display in The Innovator's Handbook. This book is pure generosity and creative gold—sweet, fun, packed with practical exercises, and layered with ways to see your world anew again."

—SAM SARRAF, *Senior Hardware Art Director at Apple*

"Innovation is often seen as mysterious and unreachable. Hussain helps finding a tangible path between the particular and the general, between one's ideas and inspirations, and between the innovative and thought-provoking and status-quo-breaking creations that can impact many. His book starts with "honoring your vision," which kicks off a clearly outlined recipes for leading to truly great results."

—SÉBASTIEN DEGUY, PhD, *Founder of Allegorithmic. Vice President, 3D & Immersive at Adobe*

"Part manifesto and part how-to, The Innovator's Handbook reminds us that creative work is multi-faceted, any idea can be approved, and the new may only be one small step away. As you invite and include diversity to all that you do -- that inspiration and wonder will drive your ideas to great heights."

—FRANS JOHANSSON, *Author of The Medici Effect*

PRAISE FOR THE INNOVATOR'S HANDBOOK

"It is a time of change - and these are the moments when innovation and design thinking can illuminate a new way of approaching and solving these problems. Not just in business and industry, but in the arts and the new mediums of digital expression that are constantly shifting. Hussain offers a unique perspective as a true creator of ideas and tireless explorer of form and visuals. I'm very excited to see Hussain adding his voice to the broader conversation of what the future holds for creatives of all types as the world and it's needs change at an exponential rate."

—*LEON IMAS, VP Design, PepsiCo*

"A great kick and spark for creators. It took me three sessions to finish this little book because it kept inspiring ideas I had to try right away."

—*DEREK SIVERS, Author + Entrepreneur*

"Hussain is one of the great creative minds that we have in North America right now. Here he's given us a behind-the-scenes look at how he designs and the various approaches and methods he uses. This outstanding book is truly for anyone in the creative industries looking for a new path to creating innovative and compelling products, services, and experiences."

—*TIM ANTONIUK, Architure Inc. + Assoc. Professor of Industrial Design, University of Alberta*

"Hussain Almossawi is one of the world's foremost authorities on creativity and the cultivation of innovative ideas. In this timeless collection of thoughtful expressions, insights, and examples, he demonstrates that innovation is the by-product of a focused, intentional effort by anyone who desires to impact the world in a meaningful way. This book will surely spark the minds of tomorrow's creative leaders."

—*JASON MAYDEN, CEO Trillicon Valley, Designer + Educator + Entrepreneur*

THE INNOVATOR'S HANDBOOK

A Short Guide to Unleashing Your Creative Mindset

Hussain Almossawi

Copyright © 2022 by **Hussain Almossawi**

All rights reserved. No part of this publication may be reproduced—mechanically, electronically, or by any other means, including photocopying—without prior written permission of the Author.

Disclaimer: To the extent permitted by applicable law, MOSSAWI STUDIOS, LLC disclaims any express or implied representation or warranty (including, without limitation, implied warranties of merchantability, of fitness for a particular purpose, or of non-infringement) related to this publication and/or its contents. By reading and/or using this publication and/or its contents and/or any data herein, user agrees that MOSSAWI STUDIOS, LLC shall not be liable for any losses arising from the use of this publication or its contents. In no event shall MOSSAWI STUDIOS, LLC, or any of its officers or representatives, be liable for any special, incidental, or consequential damages (including, without limitation, loss of profits, loss of business, loss of goodwill, loss of revenues, or loss of opportunity), whether based on breach of contract, tort (including negligence), or otherwise, whether or not MOSSAWI STUDIOS, LLC has been advised of the possibility of such damage. Additionally, no warranty may be created or extended by sales representatives or written sales materials. The contents of this publication and the results expressed therein are unique and should not be understood to apply to all.

This publication and its contents are shared for educational purposes and do not make any guarantees or warranties for their suitability or applicability to the reader. The reader is encouraged to consult with relevant professionals wherever appropriate.

Library of Congress Control Number: 2022904207

ISBN 978-1-7378508-0-9 (pbk);

Published by Mossawi Studios, LLC, Dearborn Michigan.

For more information about the **Author** and **Mossawi Studios LLC**, visit **www.mossawistudios.com**.

Printed in Bahrain

First Edition

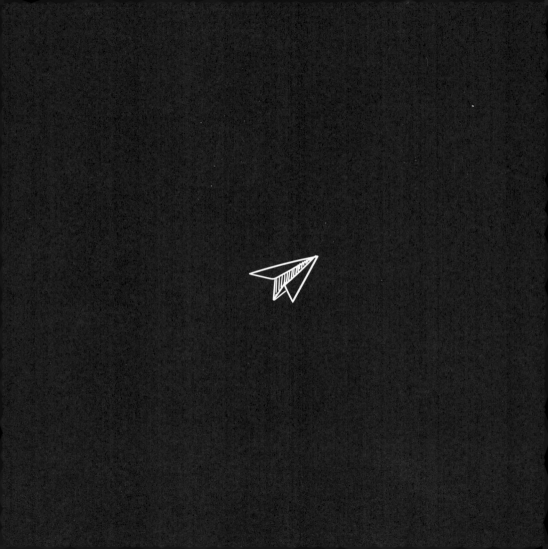

TO MY
WONDERFUL
FAMILY

THE POWER OF THE INNOVATOR .. 12
1. HONOR YOUR VISION 22
2. FOLLOW FIRST PRINCIPLES 48
3. GET ORIGINAL 76
4. THE EVOLUTION OF IDEAS 98

5. CULTIVATE CURIOSITY 112
6. BE LASER-FOCUSED 140
7. LEARN TO FAIL 154
8. ADD DIMENSION WITH DIVERSITY .. 178
9. CHALLENGE YOUR THINKING 196
10. WHAT WILL YOU INNOVATE NEXT? .. 232

Introduction
THE POWER OF THE INNOVATOR

I was inspired to write The Innovator's Handbook following talks and workshops on the power of innovation that I've presented at different design conferences around the world. I saw how engaged people across different industries were during these talks. They were always hungry for more. However, time was our biggest constraint, as it never seemed like we have enough of it.

This book collects and shares the many facets of innovation that I've gathered throughout my career as a designer and consultant for some of the world's most innovative and influential companies, like Nike, Apple, Adidas, Intel, and Ford Motor Company, and in my time as an adjunct professor at Parsons School of Design and other institutions.

My aim with this book is to shed light on different aspects of the innovation process and the innovator's mindset to equip you to do your best work. As you go through the following ideas and exercises, you will fill your toolkit with different skills and practices and learn ways to build on your creativity.

I hope this book serves as a guide
for new creatives as they begin
their own innovation journey,
no matter what discipline
they've come from.

While this book is by no means the ultimate guide to innovation, my aim is for it to spark your curiosity and get your engines started.

Innovative thinking is a requirement for success in the design industry. Yet many young designers emerge from their studies without having covered much ground in the topic. I think it's time to empower people to believe in their own abilities to innovate, no matter where they are in their careers. It doesn't matter if you're still in design school or grinding your way through your first entry-level design job: you have the power to innovate, starting now. And you have the power to become one of the greats, as well.

One of the greatest innovators of all time, Leonardo da Vinci, eloquently merged the worlds of art and science in such profound ways that his innovations and ideas are still used to this day. Four centuries after da Vinci, Thomas Edison, known for his numerous inventions in the electric industry, held more than one thousand patents.

Most notably, he brought together the components of an incandescent lamp, an electric light containing a wire filament that is heated until it glows. Edison's discovery marked the beginning of commercially produced light bulbs and changed our modern lifestyle in a major way. Without his experiments, and his many failures, Edison might not have become the household name he is today.

Margaret Knight was a prolific inventor in the late nineteenth century who long worked under the shadow of Thomas Edison. Journalists went as far as calling her Lady Edison. Born in Maine, she was still a young girl when she started working in a textile mill in New Hampshire. After seeing a fellow worker get injured by a defective piece of equipment, Knight came up with her first invention: a safety device for textile looms that forever changed the manufacturing world. Knight would register twenty-seven patents in her lifetime for inventions including shoe-manufacturing machines, a "dress shield" to protect garments from perspiration stains, a rotary engine, and an internal combustion engine. Through her focus on better efficiency and safety, she helped turn American manufacturing into a more humane world.

The Innovator's Handbook

Elon Musk, with his car company Tesla, has a similar approach to Edison, bringing electric vehicles into the mainstream and establishing a viable market. He is nearly as prolific as Edison as well. In addition to Tesla, Musk also started or co-founded financial tech company PayPal, aerospace company SpaceX, broadband internet provider Starlink, and biotech company Neuralink. Musk's journey shows us the power of constant innovation at work—all his companies have challenged the status quo and pushed the boundaries of technology and creative thinking to change society for the better.

In the above names, we see a direct path through some of the world's greatest innovations. And we see the power of inspiration and collaboration on creative evolution. All the things that have come before you exist for you to draw on, add to, and reinvent in new and better ways.

So, what's stopping you from adding your name to this list of history-making innovators?

The only way to discover the limits of the possible is to go beyond them into the impossible.

Arthur C. Clarke

1. HONOR YOUR VISION

Growing up as an aspiring designer, I was always fascinated by the groundbreaking innovations around me. I always asked myself, "Ah, why didn't I think of that?" The greatest ideas seemed to be the simplest and made the most sense, but I would never have thought of them that way, until they came to life.

The first couple of projects I completed fresh out of design school taught me a lot about the realities of the industry. Eager to succeed, I would push myself to the limit, wringing my brain dry trying to come up with the next big thing. I thought I had to invent something from scratch to succeed or achieve even a fraction of what other great innovators had, which isn't always the case.

At the time, I was framing my success in comparison. What I didn't realize is that type of thinking kept me locked in the pressure to replicate, which is different from innovating. It can be hard to be yourself and create something original if you're overly focused on trying to recreate the innovations of others.

I had to learn to trust and embrace my vision and my ideas.

I filled notebook after notebook with sketches, ideas, words, and quotes—some beautiful in their simplicity and others complex, some realistic and some crazy futuristic. Really, I jotted down whatever came to mind in the notebook I carried everywhere, a practice I still do to this day. I suggest you carry an idea book with you, too.

Real-world design work can be very rewarding and inspiring, but it can also be very overwhelming and demanding. It was during those early projects that I began to learn that there's a process and a mindset to approaching innovation. The greatest innovators have consistently applied certain practices to their work. After that, my career began to gain momentum. I felt like I had made a personal and professional breakthrough regarding how to design, how to create, and how to innovate.

While working alongside and collaborating with the minds who brought the world iPhones, Air Jordans, and Ultra Boosts, I began noticing some key concepts, methods, and mindsets these innovators shared.

It was mainly during my time interning and consulting with Nike that I learned that design is nothing without innovation. I learned that innovation, and the powerful storytelling behind it that showcases a product or idea to the world, is what drives good design and makes desirable products that everybody wants to get their hands on.

Apple co-founder Steve Jobs famously said, "We are here to put a dent in the universe." Jobs followed his vision and didn't let anyone stand in the way. "Don't let the noise of others' opinions drown out your own inner voice," he once said. "And most important, have the courage to follow your heart and intuition. They somehow already know what you truly want to become."

Far too many young designers hear the skeptics say, "It won't work" and then stop. Let the naysayers push you to prove them wrong. Let your own skepticism show you new angles on your own ideas—places to improve on, expand on, and better develop. Honor your vision and let your belief in yourself bring your ideas to life.

29

The Innovator's Handbook

BUT WHAT IS INNOVATION?

Our world is changing more rapidly than ever. To thrive in our creative pursuits, we need to keep our finger on the pulse. The creative and business climate we live in demands that we adapt on the fly, be bold in our ideas, and push the envelope to achieve innovation.

But what is innovation? Take a moment to think of your favorite brand. What draws you to them? What separates them from the rest of the pack? Real innovation takes something that already exists and reveals a new way of interacting with it, forever changing everything you *thought* you knew. Consider how fundamentally streaming services like Netflix have changed how we experience film and television, empowering us to consume stories when, where, and at the rate that we want.

But innovation is so much more than just a groundbreaking idea; it's also about execution. How will your vision come to life? How will it meet consumer needs? These are vital questions that we must ask ourselves along the way.

Adi Dassler, founder of Adidas, invented spiked shoes back in the 1920s, which became the foundation of the Adidas empire that exists today. The process of refining this idea gave Adidas its reputation for manufacturing amazing track spikes that gave athletes an advantage on the track, most notably after Adidas-wearing athletes helped the U.S. win four gold medals at the 1936 Berlin Olympics.

Being an innovator doesn't mean that every design you create will be world changing. Innovation can be as simple as improving something that already exists, and sometimes that improvement comes through simplification. In fact, innovation comes in all sizes, from a big idea in a major industry, to a small idea that grows and improves in stages, elevating both aesthetics and function. Over time, Dassler would hold more than seven hundred patents, some big, some small, some forgotten, and many that are still used today in the world of sports shoes and athletic equipment. If you can take something that people need, put your own spin on it, and somehow make it better—you have innovated.

The Innovator's Handbook

No matter the size of your idea, think big.

When you're working on smaller innovations, think about how you can be at the forefront of a significant leap in design or technology in your industry. Even better, let your creativity soar, and always be on the lookout for a radically new and different idea; something with the potential to change the world as we know it.

Craft your vision, and don't let anything stop you from realizing it to its fullest potential.

This is innovation.

BUT WHY DO WE NEED INNOVATION?

Innovation is critical to our success as creatives. We live in a globally connected world, with diverse competition and more offerings on the market in any given industry than ever before. Innovation is key to standing out and differentiating our own brand from everyone else's.

However, just because we can innovate doesn't answer the question of why innovation is necessary. The reality is that humanity has always sought ways to increase our quality of life. Innovation leads to increased effectiveness, efficiency, and enjoyment of our daily lives.

One of the most significant innovations of our time was the iPhone. I don't even need to tell you how significantly Apple changed the world with its technology. Apple showed the world something it didn't even know it needed.

The iPhone changed people's lives when it first launched and continues to do so to this day. Its popularity and global impact are a testament to its ingenwuity and essentialness.

At the time nobody asked for a mobile phone that would change how the world engaged with digital media. However, we all needed, or could benefit from, the unique aspects that made the product wildly popular—an intuitive touchscreen, faster ways to communicate and connect across the globe, the speed to reach anyone in any moment, and a seemingly endless array of applications that make our day-to-day lives easier. Imagine all that, rolled into one device. What a gift smartphones ended up being.

Innovation propels the world forward. Think of how different life is today compared to forty, thirty, or even just twenty years ago.

We have taken massive leaps and bounds in such a short amount of time, and we're just getting started. This progress was fueled by innovation.

With innovation, we have the potential to make people's lives easier and make the world a better place.

Understanding why we need to innovate can help drive our creative pursuits. When you truly grasp the idea that the next product you design may make life easier and more exciting for yourself and everyone around you, it will help propel you through trial and error, and on to the final product.

Remember, innovators create things that people won't forget. Strive to be unforgettable in all that you do.

WHY IS IT SO HARD TO INNOVATE THEN?

There's no doubt about it: innovation is not easy. Human beings have been creating since the beginning of history. Attempting to come up with something new when so much has already been done before is a challenge, which is why it's critical to rely on your unique perspective more than ever. While many people have created in the past, no one has ever seen the world from your perspective.

Innovation is also tricky because you never know just how an idea will work out until you've tried it. You may put a ton of effort and creativity into something only to realize it's not going to work as effectively as it seemed to in your mind. You must go back to the drawing board and redevelop, redefine, and reinvent your idea until it works.

If you can stay one step ahead of cultural trends and see even the most basic of everyday items—a chair, spoon, toothpick—with fresh eyes, you can bring people new ideas that will shape their experiences and better their lives.

Imagine a sports mouthguard that detects concussion-forced impacts. A spoon that reads the nutritional content of food. Gloves that detect body temperature and adjust automatically. Once you visualize how your idea will improve a product or enhance someone's daily experience, you just need to work out how to execute that vision.

Of course, it's incredibly difficult to instantaneously become a visionary—becoming an innovator doesn't happen overnight. It is important to take the time to invest in practices and methods that take will move you above and beyond your typical way of thinking about and engaging with the world. Small shifts in perspective can lead to large movements in innovation.

While becoming a visionary innovator starts with trusting yourself, your ideas, and your vision, it's a lifelong creative process that results from knowing the principles of innovation, harnessing the power of your unique creative outlook, and putting in the work. All of that takes time, but it's worth every second. The more you flex your creative muscles and gain knowledge of your craft, the more efficient you'll become.

When the going gets tough, just remember that every step forward brings you closer to becoming a better problem-solver and a more innovative thinker.

You can't solve a problem on the same level that it was created. You have to rise above it to the next level.

Albert Einstein

2. FOLLOW FIRST PRINCIPLES

Deconstruct then reconstruct—this is the cornerstone of an approach to creativity and innovation known as "first principles."

Adopted from the teachings of the Greek philosopher, Aristotle, who described it as "the first basis from which a thing is known," first principles offers one of the most effective strategies to fuel innovative thinking for groundbreaking results by breaking a whole thing down into its many parts to determine what's essential, what's extraneous, and what needs improving.

Imagine there's a sneaker in front of us. We see the laces, sole, colors, brand logo. Maybe it's wide or narrow. It could be for men, women, or unisex. Perhaps it's intended to boost performance in a certain sport. What if we break the shoe down into its individual parts, then put it together again in a totally new way?

When I was a senior designer for Adidas Advance Concepts, a team that pushed groundbreaking ideas within the brand, I was the design lead on a signature basketball shoe for NBA superstar James Harden. I travelled to Paris to partner up with designer Alexander Taylor, an amazing designer and innovator in the footwear industry.

We took Harden's existing shoes and tore them apart into different components, labelling each one and their function and displaying them out on a table—laces for a fit system, elastic band over the forefoot for fit system, leather material for durability, rubber outsole for traction, boost technology midsole for comfort, metallic logo for branding, eyelets for lacing functionality.

We then listed James's specific needs—to feel secured and locked in, to become a faster player when he accelerated, stopped, and pivoted.

Each athlete is different, but with this shoe, it was all about speed. In sports, every millisecond is accounted for, so our task was all about how we could make the athlete run faster, and how we could we make them stop and pivot in any my moment while running at full speed. James needed complete and instant control of his connection to the floor to flourish.

FIRST PRINCIPLES IN ACTION

With a clear vision and task in mind, and an existing product broken down into its core components, we started to question every single element of the existing Harden shoe. The purpose was to take each component and understand what it did and whether it got us closer or further from our final goal. We asked questions such as:

- Which parts of the shoe where unnecessary and could be gotten rid of?
- What's the purpose of each part?
- Are there better ways we could implement it?
- Does a shoe really need a lacing system?
- If not, then how else could we create a comfortable and secure fit?
- Does it really need cushioning across the entire foot?

As a result of our first principles approach, we were able to improve our design process and focus our explorations on specific components that had potential to either be replaced or removed from the shoe, in addition to introducing new components for the first time.

For example, when exploring how we could make an athlete run faster, we first looked at the basic elements of the shoe and the existing materials being used.

Part of running fast meant cutting down the weight carried to the lightest point that James felt he could operate securely and safely still. The previously designed shoe had a large amount of leather on it, which by nature is heavy. At the same time, leather is extremely durable and has a nice touch to it. It also had the athlete's logo made from small pieces of metal that were attached to the shoe.

We started looking into alternative leathers and other materials to drop some weight. That lead us to working with engineered knits, which can get extremely light, are breathable, and can be tailored specifically to an athlete's foot to help some areas of the material lock them in while other areas expand to prevent tension or tearing. That was a perfect transition. We adapted to a material that is constantly being advanced on and that quickly solved one of our problems: too much weight in the shoe.

When it came to making James stop and pivot in a split second on the court, we found his existing shoes did an amazing job. In fact, his shoe had some of the strongest traction in the market at the time. But we still questioned why the traction looked the way it did. Did we need a big piece of rubber going all the way under James's foot? Were there lighter materials and rubbers we could use? Any better traction patterns we could come up with? Those questions lead us down a rabbit hole of being able to make James stop better, and faster, but eventually it gave us new problems to think about.

Let's say a basketball player stops in an instant, which was the idea we were pushing towards. But is that a good thing? Doesn't he need an agile fit system that can lock him in yet allow him to run and move around the court freely and in full confidence? That made us question our whole approach.

Suddenly the conversation became more about a good fit system rather than making James stop and brake faster. We brought a medical doctor on board and observed foot anatomy closely, understanding how the foot and muscles move, react, and how to best keep it secure to avoid any kind of injuries.

With those insights in hand, we started to look at different ways to lace the shoe up to achieve the best and safest fit system. Should the laces go down the middle of the foot like a traditional shoe? Is it better to place them on the medial or lateral side of the shoe? Does a conventional lacing system even make sense? What if we removed the laces and reinforced it with our engineered knits that we were already considering using? What if we invented a new locking mechanism that kept the foot secured at all times? It's those questions that added value to our process and design more than anything else. They were all eye openers and made us rethink the shoe as if we were looking at shoes for the first time in our lives.

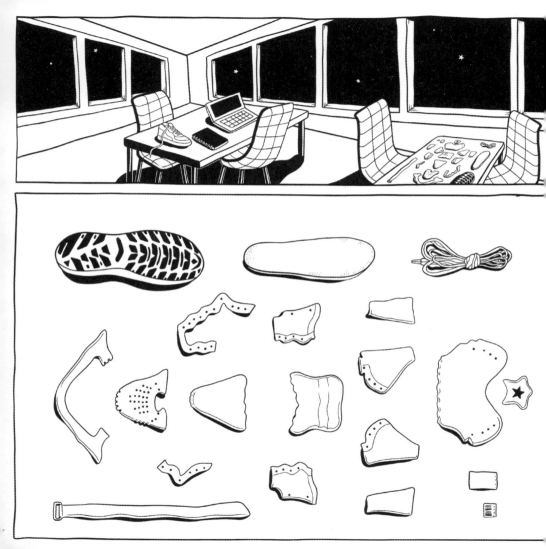

Eventually all our brainstorming pushed us towards finding answers from others who might have addressed similar solutions in different sports or other industries. For instance, how did the aerospace industry approach fit systems (laces, for us)? The same went for traction. How did companies like Michelin and Continental in the automotive industry approach grip and traction on car tires for different surfaces and innovate in the space of ground contact?

This sort of cross-pollination between industries energized us as a team. It allowed us to view those dilemmas and issues with a different lens. Not all of them worked, but that was the interesting part: we had an idea and a story, and if we believed in a direction that made sense, we would seek to validate it and prototype it, iterating over and over, testing different ways it could potentially work.

All this stemmed from our first principles approach of questioning and challenging the elements of an already widely successful basketball shoe. We were able to dive deep into every aspect of the shoe and get back to basics.

As a result, we ended up with multiple solutions for how our shoe could be different and better than it had been. During the process, we got rid of a lot of things that might have worked at one time. But with materials, technologies, and manufacturing processes advancing rapidly, new solutions that were previously unavailable had become more accessible. We designed several prototypes of the shoe that were lighter, stronger, and implemented new fit systems that had never been used before in the footwear industry.

Through our dedication to first principles thinking, we were able to truly give James a shoe that the world had never seen before.

This is first principles thinking in action. A first principles approach doesn't necessarily mean you break each object down to its molecular level, but you dig deep into its basic building block components to understand the parts of the whole. You identify what is needed and what is extraneous. Then you look outside your box for inspiration on improving those components. This type of thinking allows you to challenge and question every element until you arrive at its best iteration.

Deconstructing First Principles

Many of today's most innovative products build on products that already exist. Some designers assume that the current design is a product's best iteration. This causes them to carry those same core concepts and characteristics into the next new product they are working on. But what if some of those core concepts could be improved? What if a mistake was made early in the process that's been repeated over and over because designers assumed it was the best, or even the only, solution?

There are three key steps to a first principles approach to innovation:
1. Identify and define your assumptions about a particular idea or object.
2. Break the problem down into its most basic parts.
3. Study those parts extensively to develop new ideas and bring them together into a brand-new concept.

Rather than spending time trying to innovate a solution to a problem, first principles takes the issue and enables you to go back to the drawing board.

Let's break down each step and see how we can apply first principles to create an innovative new product.

1

Identifying and Defining Assumptions About an Idea

When first looking at a problem, it's very easy to jump headfirst into a solution without truly understanding the issue at hand. That's the equivalent of putting the cart before the horse. Rather than jumping to a solution and trying to make it fit, spend the time to identify and understand the problem, then you can consider what may not be necessary in the first place and brainstorm improvements.

Think back on the shoe example. Rather than immediately sketching out what the brand's new shoe should look like, spend time defining your assumptions before diving in. Be flexible about your assumptions: flip them around, always ask what-if questions, and let your imagination go wild. What if the laces didn't exist? What if the laces were on the inside? What if the laces were on the bottom of the shoe? And so on.

2

Breaking Down the Problem

Now that you've spent some time understanding your assumptions, it's time to get out some paper and pencils, or start up your computer if you're working in a digital product design space.

It's essential to really understand every individual part of the problem you are solving. This isn't just about breaking down the parts of a concept or product, but the ideas that originally led to those designs in the first place.

Once we break down the product into its base parts, we can analyze these elements with greater scrutiny. This allows us to see things we may not have noticed before and see new opportunities for a design that the original product missed.

3

Develop Brand-New Solutions

Now comes the fun part—taking those individual parts and constructing a solution from them.

Elon Musk is one of the most recognizable pioneers of the first principles approach to innovation and has used it in different industries both for Tesla and SpaceX. When designing the flagship Tesla Roadster, Elon Musk was told that the battery packs were expensive, costing somewhere around $600 per kilowatt hour. He was also told there was no way to get it much cheaper than that. First principles thinking first asks several questions. What is the battery made of? Where can we get those materials cheaper? Musk discovered that he could buy the elements of a battery and reconstruct it for about $80/kilowatt hour. All this stemmed from changing perspective when approaching a problem.

Suddenly, building a rocket that changed how we approached space travel was just another part of the business. For Musk, the first principles approach to design and innovation allowed him to challenge perceived notions of what's possible and led to the next stage of human spaceflight.

There are plenty of real-world examples of first principles at work. Take the Gutenberg press, which gave birth to the printing revolution and furthered the spread of information by enabling books to be produced and disseminated worldwide. The innovator himself, Johannes Gutenberg, broke the printing process down into its three most fundamental elements: paper, ink, and moving type. Taking those three elements, he combined them with the power of a screw press and the flexibility of a coin punch to create an entirely new and efficient way to print lettering onto paper.

By looking at an idea from all angles, after stripping it back to its basic elements, you can truly understand why it was created in such a way. You can see the intent behind each part, the problems it solved, and potentially find new ways of solving those same issues with a totally different solution, especially by taking advantage of newer technologies and materials.

The Innovator's Handbook

APPLYING FIRST PRINCIPLES THINKING

The first principles approach forces you to think differently about problems. It encourages questioning the assumptions that may have created those problems in the first place.

Humans are constructed to build off each other's successes and accomplishments, it takes greater vision and effort to break it all down and examine that very first block, especially when those processes and systems you're questioning are widely accepted throughout the industry as the status quo or "the way things have always been done."

As you journey through your design process, ask yourself where you find yourself getting stuck. Break down the problem into first principles and question everything. Before long, you'll start to notice new ideas and possibilities emerge as you get back to basics.

When you implement first principles thinking in your design processes, the design possibilities are ~~limitless.~~

If you want something new, you have to stop doing something old.

Peter F. Drucker

3. GET ORiGiNAL

The world of innovation and design can be sorted into two camps: those who act upon potential opportunities in the industry, and those who react and respond to changes too late.

In the corporate world, when you are surrounded by a larger, talented team, it's really easy to develop a sense of imposter syndrome. I've seen it repeatedly working in different companies, different industries, and different parts of the world. Some teams truly allow you to shine and thrive; while others push you down and make you doubt yourself, no matter how talented a creative you are.

It often has a lot to do with the way the corporate world is set-up. In many cases, it rewards the outspoken over the quiet ones, and allows egos and politics to get in the way of celebrating great ideas. This eventually pushes a lot of people to take the back seat and play it safe.

Making the jump from reacting to acting can be challenging. However, true innovators take a leader's mindset when it comes to their designs. They look beyond today's trends to tomorrow's possibilities. When you get original and learn how to act rather than react, you'll unlock the door to even greater innovative potential.

It starts with a mindset shift.

Acting – "The Leader Mindset"

While at Nike, I interviewed one of the design executives and creative directors about how they kept up with current trends and hype. His answer has stuck with me to this day. He told me that they were not concerned with what was "cool." Nike is, and always has been, an industry leader. Nike sets the tone for what people perceive as cool and creates products based on strong stories, culture, and innovation. Nike, by way of simply being Nike, had cool covered.

Taking action is the process of coming up with a unique answer to a problem, either from within yourself or based on new external insights, and leading the charge toward bettering the world. It requires original thought, and often breaks the limits of the accepted. It's not easy, yet it's something that we're all striving to do every time we set out to design.

All creative-minded people would love to lead a new idea and trend, but it's a much riskier path. It could lead to success . . . or instant failure.

To lead means to be able to think ahead of current trends. Innovators need to have the courage not only to lead others but also to step outside the norm and declare when they think something can be done better.

The way that you present your ideas is crucial. They will live or die by your ability to deliver them in an engaging manner. You must pursue what you wholeheartedly believe to be the best path, no matter how fully it shatters the norms. That requires considerable self-confidence and vision for what you are trying to bring to life.

Fortunately, we have a high risk-tolerance as creatives. We'll champion the idea over ourselves, showing the world how life could be better through innovative ideas. Seth Godin, best-selling author, marketer, and public speaker, frames it best: "The job isn't to catch up to the status quo; the job is to invent the status quo."

The most significant barrier to embracing action, beyond finding that first seed of an idea, is fear. Cultivate the mindset of a leader within yourself, and never stop pushing the envelope.

REACTING — "THE FOLLOWER MINDSET"

Reacting is on the other end of the innovator's mindset spectrum, or what I call the follower mindset. A lot of companies and brands fall into this category since they're not seen as a leading force in the industry, or they lack the confidence to show the world something new. Having a follower's mindset isn't wrong; it allows you to innovate within a much smaller box, as defined by the current leaders in that space. But it can lead to hesitation, the loss of ideas to competitors, and a stagnant brand.

In my time with various brands and companies, I've seen unique ideas die, only to see them resurrected a few months later—created by leading competitors. You snooze, you lose! The success of the idea then makes everyone wish they had acted sooner! Not only did I see this in product design companies, but I also saw it when I worked in advertising.

While action is dynamic, reaction is passive. Reaction can be used as a runway, inspiring you to fly to fresh ideas and see things differently.

However, it often results in lazy thinking, repetition, stagnation, and confining yourself within a bubble defined by what you are reacting to. You may retain the skills to improve things, but by continually reinterpreting others' ideas, you can lose the touch of originality. Furthermore, by waiting for the next big thing to happen, you can miss the spark of action that lies within you, reducing your effectiveness as a creative-minded person.

We can see this in action when observing big brands and companies from the sidelines. Adidas, for example, saw widespread success when they launched their very innovative Ultra Boost line that featured an extremely soft and comfortable sole made up of small palettes compressed into the shape of a sole.

Following its huge success, the same design language, aesthetic, and idea started to show up in other competitor brands under different names, with small twists or changes. Some brands, too lazy to bother adding their own flavor, simply threw a new name and logo on essentially the same shoe!

The same battles can be seen between Apple and Samsung, Coke and Pepsi, BMW and Audi, and other rivals. The moment one brand does something well, it provokes the other to react with their own "version" of it.

There's nothing wrong with innovating against your rival. However, this cat-and-mouse game of catchup with your competitor will often keep you in second place. While you are busy catching up, they are busy thinking about their next big move.

89

The Innovator's Handbook

SHOULD YOU ACT OR REACT?

The Innovator's Handbook

Acting and reacting don't only happen between rival companies. I've seen this tug-of-war play out between departments within the same brand!

For instance, you could have a single eyewear company with two different design teams designing different kinds of products—one for eyeglasses and the other for sunglasses—engaged in this same back-and-forth. One of the teams is always leading and setting the bar high, while the other is always trying to keep up.

I've also seen it play out on a team level. Some individuals like to go all out on creativity and dream big, while others look around them seeking inspiration and thought-starters, which is the whole idea behind collaborating in teams. With the right team and balance, wonderful ideas can be born out of multiple chain reactions back and forth between team members.

A designer must constantly walk the fine line between acting and reacting. It may seem difficult at first, but this state is ideal because it is in the balance that innovation can arise. Later chapters will look at this balance in detail and how you can walk the tightrope successfully.

As a creative, you will understand that the most significant rewards come from recognizing a trend before it becomes a trend. Serial entrepreneur Mike Michalowicz talks about this concept in his book, Surge, and how entrepreneurs (and designers) who best catch and ride the wave of a trend profit, while those who react often make money but will never outcompete a company that reacted before the trend took off.

REACTION

ACTION

The Innovator's Handbook

Of course, he also talks about how this concept is, at its core, extremely difficult to live out consciously. Not every business is the next Nike or Amazon. You can't always forecast what will take off, whether you innovate or reimagine a new product or service. You can certainly learn to see which ideas have potential, but no designer, entrepreneur, or investor knocks it out of the park every time.

You need to act and react simultaneously—act to push for new ideas and solutions; react to the things that inspire you and change your perspective. Action and reaction are the yin and yang of innovation that work seamlessly together. When you both act and react, you can become a great innovator with the vision to see both sides of every process and harness the capabilities on both sides.

Be wise and be bold. Know your stuff, and you'll rise to new heights that you never thought were possible!

Innovation is seeing what everybody has seen and thinking what nobody has thought.

Dr. Albert, Szent- Györgyi

4. THE EVOLUTION OF IDEAS

With first principles thinking, we discussed an approach for generating new, innovative ideas that, when used effectively, can change industries, and make an impact on the world. However, coming up with an idea is only the beginning.

The next step is to evolve that idea into what it's truly meant to become.

I've worked on hundreds of conceptual projects in the footwear, automotive, and product design spaces; the whole idea behind concepts is to kind of go blue sky and design a vision without constraints, setting a North Star for inspiration in the direction you want to head. Concepts are great for creating hype for the designer or brand and giving their work more exposure and visibility to the public. But the downside of concepts, whether on the level of an individual designer or a multibillion-dollar company, is that they sometimes create buzz but don't go anywhere after.

Concepts will always remain concepts.

Their ultimate impact is drawing a north star to be inspired from and excited by. Real products make change and become the innovations that stand out and continue to evolve. The challenge for most creatives is turning their idea into a reality. Once you've accomplished that, the next challenge is to continually improve on that reality.

While at Adidas, I worked closely on the Adidas LightStrike, a super-light midsole that provides the perfect balance of lightweight cushioning and responsiveness. It's a foam that's perfectly tuned for explosive movements, and it got adapted into basketball, running, and shoes for different sports. The LightStrike foam had a distinctive aesthetic of being multi-faceted and geometric, which allowed it to catch light and change color as the athlete moved, enriching the shoe with the visual illusion of speed and grace.

Across the many shoes it was used, and over the years that it was implemented, it's main aesthetic never changed. The faceted faces changed size, shape, depth, and color, but it always retained the same aesthetic, which made it easily recognizable and iconic. Rather than hitting the drawing board and reinventing the wheel every time, we used what we had as a starting point and continued to improve on an already impressive product.

NURTURE, NURTURE, NURTURE

In many ways, your ideas are like a child. You have to help them grow up and become strong enough to stand on their own. To do this, you must constantly engage with your project or idea. You need to take the time to ask yourself what needs improvement and how you can improve it. You need to build upon the idea until it's unique and revolutionary.

This part of the innovation process may seem simple, yet many people underestimate or entirely forget about it. They immediately go into execution mode without taking the time needed to produce something truly remarkable. However, the evolution of an idea is just as important as the original idea. The more you work with it, the better it becomes, and the more it starts to make sense.

Respected architect Frank Gehry speaks of the evolution of an idea as the process of "going with it." He describes the creative process as one where the designer works intuitively to create something, often not knowing exactly where the idea is heading. The designer just lets the creative idea move forward naturally. He trusts it, does not overthink it, but goes with the flow until he gets somewhere amazing that he could have never planned or predicted.

Amazon is a great example of how an idea can evolve. Founder Jeff Bezos launched his empire by selling books online. The concept was simple: give people a fast and effective way to buy new and used books over the internet. Amazon's initial success soon led Bezos to start expanding his business model, creating an entire online marketplace where businesses big and small could sell practically everything under the sun.

Today, Amazon is an integral part of everyday life—from original content creation, to cloud computing, to online marketplaces, and more.

And Bezos? His willingness to continue evolving his original idea has made him a household name worldwide.

Facebook was no different than Amazon. It first started out as a social media platform targeted for college students only. If you had a university email, you could sign up. As it found traction and popularity amongst college students, they started to open it up to the entire public while constantly improving their features and studying their user base as their product and platform evolved.

It's the same if you look at physical products in any industry. Compare the first iPhone to the latest version. You can see a nice progression from one to another, an evolution that instantly makes sense, even though the first model and the one produced ten or fifteen years later might look and feel totally different. Still, there's a logic to how the product got *from there to here*.

Author Henry James likens the evolution process to having a big stick in a deep barrel. You can't see what is in the barrel, but as you keep at it and continue to stir, a great idea rises to the surface—often unexpectedly.

As an innovator and designer, you must be willing to let the idea evolve and grow, never knowing how or where it will end up. The final result may be an idea you never anticipated, but it is precisely what it needs to be. Any project can forever evolve and improve—there's no question about that. The only thing that makes us push the stop button on creative evolution is time and deadlines.

Celebrate your wins, and feel proud of your accomplishments, but just like with sports, there's always next season, which is a new battle and new challenge for you to shine in again. Take the success you've had in past years, the projects that were "finished" by constraints like deadlines. Return to those ideas and see if they can be further developed and applied to future projects as well.

There's a way to do it better — find it.

Thomas A. Edison

5. CULTIVATE CURIOSITY

Once, during a conversation with Tinker Hatfield, VP of Design at Nike, he advised me to "be a sponge." As a sponge, you are absorbing as much as you can from everything around you; everything you see, hear, smell, feel, and taste enters your creative space.

Approaching the world this way opens the limiting box we sometimes put ourselves in and allows us to approach things with a fresh perspective. That single piece of advice has elevated my design process and approach towards creativity ever since.

When I was working on a Visual Effects project for Intel, the same rules of curiosity applied in the digital space. My task was to create an Art Film that evoked different emotions through the visual experiences evoked, the sounds used, and the colors employed. With my VFX and CGI hat on, and as I was looking for inspiration, I was always hyper alert and curious about the physical properties of everything around me, what they looked like and how they acted.

What would they feel like? How would they react when interacting with other objects? it is it sharp or smooth? Would it float? Would it break, tear, and so on?

Looking at everyday objects with a deeper sense of curiosity helps us translate the physical to the digital space. Knowing how things should be or act in reality opens the door to hack that reality and defy all the rules of physics in our creations and designs. With Intel, one of the experiences in the project was a concrete floor, with a perfect circle cut out in the middle of it filled with hundreds of air bubbles, as a pendulum swiveled on top of the bubbles, they would inflate and massively grow, creating a magnetic force effect as they chased after the pendulum. Suddenly you can challenge the mind and eye to create something totally new and unexpected and deliver a truly unique experience.

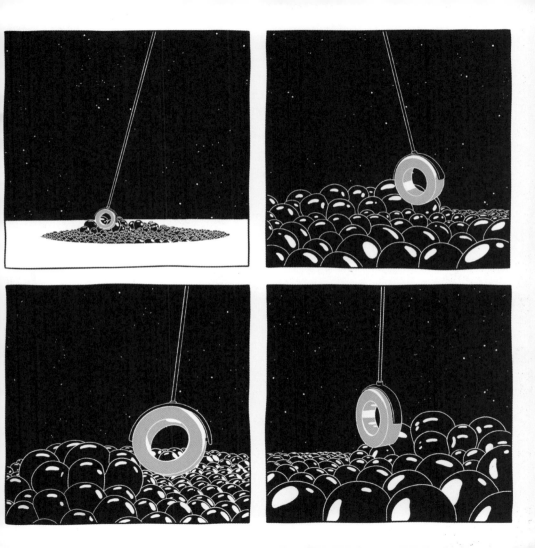

Brooklyn, New York is a melting pot of creatives. Being based there provided a landscape for inspiration with its rich culture and history. Whether it was enjoying the art scene on the streets, highly curated shows at museums like MOMA, watching the Knicks play at Madison Square Garden, or checking out a pick-up game at one of the many street courts around the city—inspiration and curiosity-firing moments were everywhere.

No matter where you live or where you are, there is always something to be curious about. Always lead with why when observing the world around you, having conversations with others, or exploring subjects that interest you. Always putting your observer hat on will make you instantly value everything around you, allow you to make new connections around how things work, and give you a deeper level of connection to your environment.

117

The Innovator's Handbook

How Curiosity Drives Innovation

The Innovator's Handbook

In his notebooks, Leonardo da Vinci analyzed, examined, and questioned almost everything he saw in the world around him, asking questions like, "What does the tongue of a woodpecker look like?" or "Why is the sky blue?"

Leonardo was a total sponge.

Curiosity to that level reminds me of Ryan Babineaux's observations in his book, Fail Fast, Fail Often, where he notices that children are great teachers of innovation. According to Babineaux, children constantly bombard their parents and other adults with questions that seem basic and unimportant in a busy world. Yet it's these questions that showcase the innocent curiosity that can ultimately lead our innovation to new discoveries that expand our understanding of the universe and our place in it!

Speaking of children, let's go back to the world of animation.

When Pixar was first founded, the teams often engaged in what is known as "question storming." You may have heard of brainstorming, but rather than trying to get to ideas out of nowhere, question storming involves asking questions that provoke creative thinking.

According to Ed Catmull, who previously led Pixar and the author of Creativity Inc., this process helped Pixar's creative minds stay curious, gain new perspectives, and find innovative answers to tough questions, rather than jumping straight to solutions.

In a similar vein, Hal Gregersen, author of Questions Are the Answer, offers a method called "question bursts," which encourage thinkers to ask as many questions as possible and always stay curious to find the best way forward.

Being an innovator means needing a constant stream of unparalleled inspiration. Finding this kind of inspiration on a continuous basis is one of the biggest challenges you are likely to face. Luckily, sources of inspiration are all around us; we just need to shape our perception so that we can become a sponge and soak it all up.

Living life in this way means you will never let an opportunity to innovate pass you by. Inspiration often comes from unlikely sources, and we can miss it if we're not willing to keep an open mind. Don't lose your next great idea just because you're holding yourself back by staying in your comfort zone and restricting yourself to what is currently shaping your ideas.

CURIOSITY IN ACTION

The Innovator's Handbook

In 2001, when designers at Nike were looking for the next great innovation, they put their curiosity to work. That curiosity led them to Stanford University, where they noticed university runners racing barefoot. After asking the coaches why they did that, the team discovered that the human foot offered a more effective strike and flex without a shoe.

As they dove further into their discovery, they found that runners who trained barefoot enjoyed more balance, strength, and flexibility. This led them to design a groundbreaking shoe—the Nike Free—which offered the benefits of running barefoot while protecting the foot with style and support.

Another prime example of curiosity in action is The Eastgate Centre in Harare, Zimbabwe. This building is the largest office and shopping complex in Zimbabwe, yet it has no air conditioning installed. Rather than use up energy to power cooling systems, architect Mick Pearce and Arup Engineers utilized the power of biomimicry to create the world's first self-cooling building.

The Eastgate Center remains temperature regulated year-round while using far less energy in an incredible way. They used Zimbabwean masonry techniques and the mounds of African termites as inspiration! The architects asked the right questions to discover how they could solve the architectural problem, and they found the answer from two very different sources. In fact, you'd be surprised at how many answers to our problems can be found in nature, it's the perfect and most sustainable blueprint for many ecosystems, and it's right before our very eyes—if we are willing to ask the right questions!

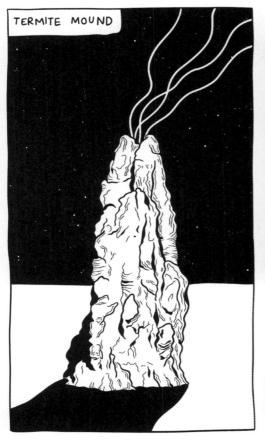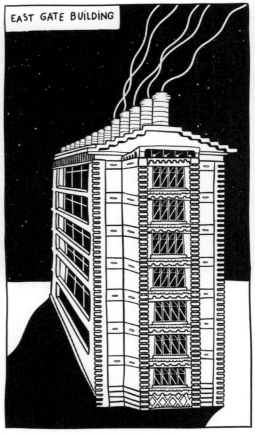

HOW DO YOU DESIGN A BUILDING THAT COOLS ITSELF?

HOW TO BE A CURIOUS SPONGE

The Innovator's Handbook

As you can see, curiosity is an incredibly powerful mindset for an innovator to cultivate. So how do you follow in the footsteps of those we admire in our world? It starts with becoming a curious sponge.

Here are a few tips to be more curious:

1

Look Around

The world is so diverse, and inspiration can be found everywhere. If you don't see it, you're just not looking hard enough. Open your eyes, and work on fostering an open mindset that seeks a fresh perspective on everyday things. The more you cultivate this mindset, the easier you will find inspiration throughout your day.

2

Be Open-Minded

Absorb every experience that comes your way and strive to see the world from different points of view. Try different ways of doing things. Switch up your routine. Do whatever it takes to keep your perspective fresh.

3

Get Curious

After you start to look around you and open your mind to new possibilities, get curious about what you are seeing. One of the essential qualities of an innovator is the ability to look at life from many angles. Cultivating a curious mindset will greatly serve us in our goal to innovate. Your evolving mindset will breathe new life into your work and help you create truly unique things.

4

Push Boundaries

Don't stay within your comfort zone of what is familiar to you and what you have done in the past. Instead, strive to create something new every time. By pushing your own boundaries and going further than you ever have, you will reach new heights of creativity and discover ideas you may not have thought of before.

PROTECT YOUR WONDER

Many of the advances that we take for granted were driven by those who were willing to ask simple questions that others may have seen as foolish.

In his book Invent & Wander, Walter Isaacs reflects on how we often lose our "childlike wonder," noting that many of the great thinkers and visionaries he studied retained a sense of awe and wonder at the world around them. Many of us lose this essential skill, choosing instead to become adults who stop asking "silly questions."

Sadly, as adults, we're often taught to ignore the "unimportant" wonders and mysteries of the world. Yet the great thinkers of our world, innovators like da Vinci, were able to unlock greater innovations because they were unwilling to outgrow their wonder years.

When did we stop being amazed by the small, magical phenomena of our everyday lives? Simply listen to the questions children ask about the inner workings of things all around them: "Why is the grass green?" "Why are trees so tall?" "Where does the moon go during the day?"

Have you outgrown your "wonder years?" Don't worry, you can regain that childlike wonder once more—it just takes being a bit more spongey. Decouple from the notion of already knowing things or not needing to know. Wander into the unknown and get curious about everything you encounter. It may be the key to unlocking your true innovation potential!

137

The Innovator's Handbook

Learning and innovation go hand in hand. The arrogance of success is to think that what you did yesterday will be sufficient for tomorrow.

William Pollard

6. BE LASER-FOCUSED

While working at Adidas on the design of James Harden's second signature shoe (the shoes he wore when he won his first MVP award in 2018) I was designing alongside design director Jesse Rademacher. Jesse had each designer bring their expertise to a different part of the shoe, ending up with a product that looked good and, most importantly, did what it was supposed to do.

I was primarily responsible for designing the outsole—in non-footwear terms, the bottom part with the traction pattern. Being laser-focused on the outsole, we worked from data captured from Harden's foot and his specific movements on the court. We created designs that responded to different pressure points on his foot and designed the traction in a way that would allow him to stop faster with more control, giving him one less thing to worry about while on the court.

The outcome was a success—James had one of his best seasons of his career and won the MVP (most valuable player) award for that year. Of course, as a designer, it's never fair to take credit for an athlete's hard work and skills, but it's a wonderful moment to celebrate and recognize that you played a part off the court.

It was incredible to see how Jesse approached the project. "Always be laser-focused on one thing when you are innovating," he told me. I've since re-implemented Jesse's advice on many different projects throughout my career.

In the footwear industry, we often design under overarching themes that our teams are tasked with solving and innovating—from creating a more flexible and lightweight shoe, to one that provided better traction and construction. Having innovation goals helps to identify different themes to solve. However, it only works when goals are isolated and focused on.

This will allow you to solve one very specific problem at a time rather than distracting yourself with myriad ideas and potential outcomes.

Phil Knight, the co-founder of Nike, in his book, Shoe Dog, shares the struggles Nike had when they first released the Nike Tailwinds. It was the first shoe that featured Nike Air, their new groundbreaking innovation at the time that put airbags in the soles, giving the runner extra comfort by making them feel like they were running on air. Instead of focusing on that one huge innovation, they had twelve different innovations going on in the same shoe at the same time, which led to dilution, underperformance, and feature failure. Ultimately, it led to the airbags blowing up.

As Phil puts it, they were just demanding a lot from a single pair of shoes, and it would have been better if they put twelve unique innovations in twelve unique shoes. Air is still one of Nike's greatest innovations to this day and can be found in many lifestyle and performance shoes. It has become a story and selling point. It was also a learning experience about the importance of focus for one of the world's most innovative companies.

There comes a moment when you begin to feel the rush of momentum. You will begin to sense that you are pushing the limits on a single idea or concept and that your ideas are starting to take shape.

This is the magic of being laser-focused—as you develop each unique idea, you can then bring them together into a brand-new concept and find a new way forward where others haven't thought to look. You'll find yourself experimenting with more new concepts and unlocking even greater innovation. The best approach is often to deliver one laser-focused solution at a time. By staying laser-focused on one outcome at a time, you're able to stay on track and build a story that brings a consumer along in your journey as your product, idea, or design evolves.

But how do you know whether you are laser-focused?

1

You Are Open to New Ideas About a Single Idea

Focusing on too many different aspects of your work will cause you to be just okay with multiple things without truly changing anything. Home in on one specific idea and work on innovating it. Innovating one thing at a time is the most efficient way of moving forward. Trying to do everything at once will quickly become messy and out of control.

2

You Can Dream Up the Unexpected

It's easy to lose track of your progress if you don't have a strong vision for what you are trying to accomplish. You can quickly become complacent, settling for the same work you always do instead of pushing forward. With tunnel-vision focus on your end goal, you can push past what you are currently capable of and really innovate the idea at hand.

3

You Can Push Beyond the Expected

Think about what you want to accomplish as an innovator. Conceptualize your biggest goals and envision them as reality before they even happen. Being able to visualize your goals becoming realities will drive you towards accomplishing them. If you don't find the confidence to believe that they can really happen, they never will.

Many of today's leading companies have become household names because they were laser-focused on solving a single problem. Uber focused on the smartest and most effective way to get from A to B without a car and developed a platform and ecosystem around that singular focus. Airbnb focused entirely on what it means to have a home anywhere you go in the world and started thinking of innovative ways to offer accommodation beyond staying at a hotel. Ikea was always focused on bringing well designed, smart, and low-cost furniture to people all around the world, and even though they have expanded into creating electronics or tiny homes, they are still staying true to their core focus, which is allowing them to innovate and create on different levels.

Define your innovation story by taking every idea as far as it can go. Then watch as you create something truly remarkable in your field.

The Innovator's Handbook

I'm as proud of many of the things we haven't done as the things we have done. Innovation is saying no to a thousand things.

Steve Jobs

7. LEARN TO FAIL

Ever since I was a kid, one of my lifelong dreams as a designer has been to work for some of the biggest sports brands in the world.

I used to run an online community called SLAM 3. It was a message board with everything basketball. We had a crew of about twenty designers from all over the world. We would design desktop wallpapers for NBA players out of true passion and love for the sport. None of us knew each other, but we were united by our passion for design.

That was the kind of kid I was. I still remember an essay we had to write in high school about our dream job. I wrote about fusing my love of sports and design and working for some of the greats. I imagined what it would be like to design for the likes of Nike, Adidas, and Puma.

Coming from Bahrain, a tiny island from the other side of the globe, I carried my big dreams and aspirations with me around the world as I attended the University of Illinois to pursue my BFA in Graphic Design.

Little did I know about the struggles that would face me along the way. Working for the big brands I had dreamed of was almost impossible given that I was only here on a student visa, and I really knew nothing at the time about what it took to work in the United States.

After graduating from college, I applied over and over again to these companies before I got anyone's attention. Being a foreign student studying in the U.S. didn't really make it any easier. I dealt with more than eighty rejections! By the end of it, I think all the HR folks knew me far too well! However, it was during those rejections that I learned a valuable lesson about "failure" and the importance of rejection.

I chose to work to find my points of weakness and improve. Whether it was my craft, portfolio, or thinking process, I used each "failure" to learn and sharpen my craft as a designer. After a few years of trying to break into the sporting industry, and rigorously improving my craft and skillsets—all while finding the best way to get my foot in the door as an international non-U.S.-based designer—my dream finally came true.

Eventually, I ended up working for each one of those brands I used to dream about, and many others as well. Some of them I still consult with to this day. However, it wouldn't have happened if I hadn't learned how to fail and grow from rejection. Where would I be if I'd thrown in the towel? Just another kid who wrote a high school essay about a dream they never reached.

In his book Failing Forward, author and leadership expert John C. Maxwell reflects on the unexpected gift of failure. Many times, failures happen due to circumstances outside of our control. When we understand this, we stop allowing failures to define our work. We realize we don't have to blame ourselves. Instead, we take responsibility for coming up with a solution.

One of the projects that I am most proud of in my career is the nCycle—a futuristic electric bike that showcased this idea of failing forward. Creating the nCycle was a real challenge, both from a design and an engineering standpoint. The way the frame is designed and constructed is different than any other standard bike, which gives it its strength and aesthetic beauty.

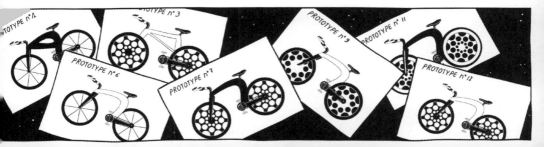

It took my design team many rounds at the drawing board to create the final version of the nCycle. We found ourselves continuously modifying our design to build a working prototype that wouldn't lose its aesthetic. Our goal was to add unbeatable strength to the frame so it would remain strong and lightweight while looking great.

The final nCycle emerged after about eight prototypes over the course of two years. After our initial failure, we could have simply given up and accepted that it was only possible on paper. However, we took each failure as an opportunity to grow, learn, and reiterate our innovation to produce an iconic electric bike that created worldwide buzz, from trade shows, to museums, to design venues.

When teaching design classes, I enjoy walking my students through a useful thought experiment about success and failure. Imagine that you are sitting down twenty years from now to write a book about all your successes and accomplishments. Now imagine how boring that book would be if there wasn't a single failure or struggle that pushed you to become the successful person you are. There would be no tension, no conflict, no character development. It's those struggles and failures that build us into who we become. Without the struggle, is a story even a story?

Failure isn't the end of the world, and don't expect to come up with great ideas and solve big problems on the first go. It takes patience and resilience. Ask any great business leader or entrepreneur, and they will point you to the moments in their lives when they faced the decision of whether to give up or press ahead despite the difficulty. You can get lucky sometimes, and the more you train yourself and perfect your process to look through problems, the faster you get and the more you enjoy the journey.

Don't hide or run from your failures or rejections. Instead, distill them down to their most valuable parts and allow them to become the fuel for the next iteration of your idea.

Look at them as life lessons. As twentieth-century author William Marston referred to it, find how you can "draw dividends from failure."

The success stories that came out of failures are endless and all around us, no matter what profession or industry turn to. Imagine if J.K. Rowling had given up on her literary pursuits when editor after editor refused to publish the Harry Potter series. Or what if Walt Disney, who was let go from his job at the Kansas City Star newspaper for what editors said was an apparent lack of imagination, had stopped creating. Or imagine if Michael Jordan stopped playing basketball because he was cut from his high school varsity team.

James Dyson, founder of Dyson Vacuums, started out his journey in the 1970s with the idea of using cyclonic separation as an alternative solution to vacuum cleaner dust bags that would get clogged by dust and reduce the suction power. His prototypes failed, one after the other, but 5,127 prototypes later, he finally succeeded and launched his first vacuum cleaner in 1983, the G-Force Cleaner. His new invention became an instant hit in Japan, where he launched it. When he brought it back home to the United Kingdom, it got rejected by every single manufacturer as it was a bagless vacuum cleaner and could potentially disturb the ongoing business of the replaceable dust bag market. Here James's failure was due to forces outside his control, which is often the case.

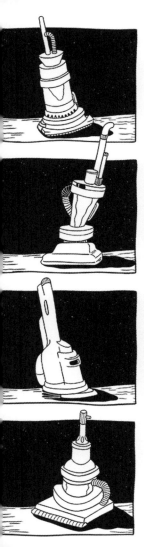

James set on his own and launched his own manufacturing company, Dyson Ltd, which is now one of the top selling vacuum manufacturers of all time. His company is considered one of the leading and most innovative vacuum cleaner brands. In addition, they've expanded into other products with their innovative mindset, such as hair dryers, fan-less fans, and lighting systems.

Another great example that started out as an ultimate failure was bubble wrap, now famous for its omnipresence in the packing and shipping industry. Two engineers, Marc Chavannes and Al Fielding, invented bubble wrap in the 1960s as a new textured wallpaper, but that failed pretty miserably, and that idea never made it. They started to think of more than four hundred ways they could re-purpose and use this great material they had.

The next idea they brought to market with it as a greenhouse insulation, yet that proved to be ineffective and unsuccessful, too. Without giving up to their failures, they introduced it as an effective packaging material, and it was only when IBM had just released the IBM 1401 computer, with fragile parts that needed extra care when being shipped, that bubble wrap found its way into one of the most effective packaging materials ever. After that, everything else was history, and bubble wrap became the world's most efficient and used material for packaging—and a favorite stomp-able toy for kids around the world as well.

Consider these three ways in which your failures can lead to successful innovation:

169

The Innovator's Handbook

1

Every Failure Is a Lesson and Chance to Improve

With every failure comes the opportunity to learn and improve. We can use our failures as a springboard to our next great innovation.

Seeing how something doesn't work has a funny way of showing us how it could work. We can work hard and see that idea through, or, if our idea doesn't work, we could discover a new idea and repeat the process. It can be a long and sometimes frustrating process, but our efforts will not have been in vain when we find what works.

2

Your Failures Are a Success Story in the Making

Think about it this way: one day, when you write the story of your successful career, imagine how boring it would be if you never experienced failure. Your greatest success is often spawned from your greatest failure.

Here is the ultimate takeaway: if we aren't willing to adapt how we do things to the changing ways of the world around us, we won't find longevity in what we do.

3

Your First Try May Not Be Perfect and That's Okay

Your first idea may not be perfect, but if you don't try again, your dream will never become a reality. If you believe in your dreams, don't just talk the talk, but also walk the walk, no matter what it takes.

Take notes and reflect on each iteration of your process and never stop learning how to fail forward. Your failures may just be the doorway to your true innovation—one you never saw coming.

173

The Innovator's Handbook

Chuck Jones was known for his animation works with Looney tunes and said it best: "You have a million bad drawings in your pencil, and your job as an artist is to get them out so the good ones can follow."

Embrace failure. Failing means gaining knowledge and experience. You can innovate faster when you can move past your loss, grow from it, and try again. This cycle defines the life of an innovator.

But how do we accept failure in our work? We live in a society that promotes self-reliance and demands performance. How do we look past that and develop the understanding that we can never attain perfection?

As innovators, we would be well served to take a lesson from the Japanese concept of Kintsugi (継ぎ). By taking shards of once-beautiful pottery and rejoining them with golden filaments, these artists take an original idea and give it new life and meaning with caring hands.

The result is something far more exquisite than ever thought possible.

There is no innovation and creativity without failure. Period.

Brené Brown

8. ADD DIMENSION WITH DIVERSITY

The Innovator's Handbook

Being a designer, or a creative of any discipline, often entails working in solitude without a lot of outside input until your work is judged by the client. But a great idea only goes so far. When your work is developed without other contributing voices, the end result can often fall short. Diversifying our environment opens us up to greater opportunities—if we are willing to let down our guard and sacrifice our pride.

I have had the incredible opportunity to work with diverse teams. Many of my greatest experiences have come from being on teams with individuals from wildly different cultures, religions, languages, and more.

During my time at EA Sports, I worked on the FIFA '15 game with an amazingly diverse team, as diverse as the soccer teams themselves that FIFA celebrates. As a designer, getting to know each team member's personal workflow and thought process was inspiring and beneficial to my own craft.

Sure, I had my own personal design aspirations and thoughts when it came to the game, but even my greatest ideas paled in comparison to what that team was able to bring to life together.

Even during lunch breaks, spending time with the team and playing a soccer or basketball matches on campus subconsciously affected our work and chemistry. Whether it was the humor, sarcasm, attitude, cultural differences, or just their day-to-day, it all opened my perspective and appreciation of diversity.

This dynamic also created a pool of diverse and positive energy that allowed us to push out great work while being exposed to new views, understandings, and capabilities.

Fine dining provides a great illustration of diversity-led innovation. Many chefs will tell you that they love to hire individuals from different kitchens, as they bring with them new and exciting perspectives. Let's say you own an Italian restaurant and employ two chefs who are trained and experienced in Italian cuisine. In general, their take on style, flavor, and presentation will be somewhat similar.

Now imagine that you introduce a Japanese chef to the team. Suddenly, new ideas and flavor combinations spring forth as they bring their unique experience and expertise to your Italian restaurant. Imagine upending the culinary world with a sushi pasta roll or a zesty Asian-inspired cannoli!

Now repeat the process and bring in an African or a Middle Eastern chef. Suddenly, the possibilities for creative dishes grow exponentially as you mix different ingredients, flavors, plating, techniques, and more. That is the power of diversity at work!

In his book The Medici Effect, author Frans Johansson reveals how the famous Medici family brought people from different walks of life to Florence with one goal—to help in its cultural development.

The culture rewarded and celebrated those who became masters in different skills, and as people from different disciplines started working together, so did their ideas, talents, and skillsets, where blurring the lines between different disciplines became the norm. The result? The wave of art, design, and technological advancement we now know as the Renaissance.

A perfect example of the Medici effect at work is found in the life of Steve Jobs, an innovator who advocated living life to the fullest and showcased that passion across his work and life. In addition to his exemplary obsession with pushing the envelope of technology, Jobs was also known to frequently remove himself from work to immerse himself in art, culture, and spirituality. These diverse experiences allowed him and his creative teams to bring to life the sleek, innovative Mac computers that surpassed anyone's wildest imagination.

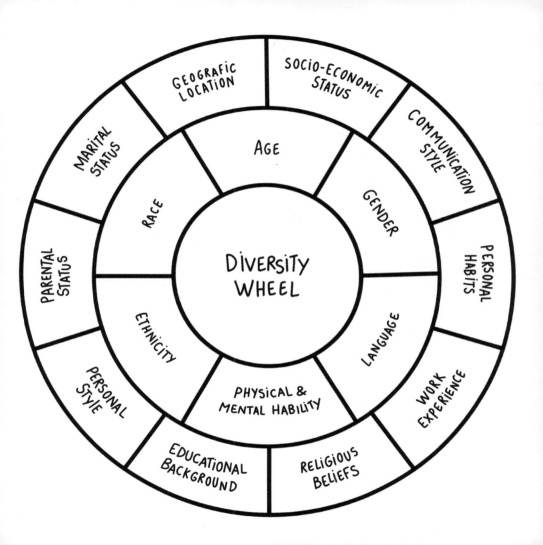

How Creators Can Use Diversity to Drive Innovation

In his book Wisdom of Crowds, author James Surowiecki puts the need for widening perspectives at the forefront of true innovation. He argues that true diversity can only emerge when disagreement is allowed space to operate in design. While compromise can be helpful, it can also hinder innovation if sought only to avoid conflict.

Here are some tips to help you create more innovative products with diversity in mind:

1

Work with People of Diverse Backgrounds and Experiences

Even if you are a "solopreneur," you will find yourself working with—or for—other teams. There is an unspoken assumption that the people working together will share similar cultures, experiences, and backgrounds.

While it makes sense to gravitate towards those who are like us, this leads to a hidden effect that holds back some of the best innovations. Be proactive about finding individuals to work with who are different from you in their background, personality, expertise, goals, and experiences.

As Surowiecki puts it: "Diversity and independence are important because the best collective decisions are the product of disagreement and contest, not consensus or compromise."

There's the key—innovation arises when you aren't starting with compromise but are instead bringing the power of competitive creativity together in one beautiful recipe.

2

Work With People You May Disagree With

Here's a tough one—but who said innovation was easy?

Diversity is not just about culture or experience. It's also about people who will challenge your thoughts, beliefs, and goals. If you have the opportunity to work with someone who is completely against your idea (perhaps they want something very different), then consider it a blessing before you assume it's a curse.

Now, tread lightly. There is a fine line between choosing not to work with negative people who kill any room for hope or optimism and avoiding those who genuinely disagree for the sake of achieving a great idea. These are two completely different mindsets and intents.

While those who are negative for negativity's sake are innovation-killers, those who genuinely want to play a beneficial devil's advocate can be your greatest assets.

3

Use the Power of Story to Unleash Diversity

As you seek to increase the diversity of thought in your innovation, don't forget the critical tenet of Johansson's The Medici Effect: The more diverse our teams are, the more diverse and innovative our ideas will become.

As you innovate, don't forget that you are working with other individuals with their own unique needs, ideas, and expertise. When you work alongside others in a diversified way, you take their combined stories and use them to your advantage to dream and develop together.

Never underestimate the power of story at the heart of diversity. In his work Lead With A Story, Paul Smith explains that storytelling is a great way to build and unleash a diverse team. There's no debate that diverse teams outperform homogeneous ones, so it's important to diversify your team's skills and experiences.

You may have the resources, the drive, and the experience—but are you optimizing these to achieve peak performance? Consider leading with the story and let the skills of your diverse team drive innovation in new ways.

Diversity within teams helps drive innovation and leads to products and ideas that shape the world in new and exciting ways. Will you take the risk to increase your diversity? Your ability to innovate may depend on it!

Innovation is taking two things that already exist and putting them together in a new way.

Tom Freston

9. CHALLENGE YOUR THINKING

There are many practical exercises and approaches towards coming up with creative ideas. I have hand-selected my favorite ones, which I have both taken part in and observed from some of the biggest and most innovative companies in the world. The following exercises are designed to help spark your creativity while brainstorming, so don't hold back. Let your imagination run free!

There are no right or wrong answers; your own creativity is the only limit. See what works best for you, and hopefully, it will help you the next time you're brainstorming your next big idea. The following exercises can be performed either on your own or in a group setting. Feel free to try both, as that can expand your horizons and bring about even greater innovation!

Are you ready to explore your creativity?

1

Forced Connections

A big part of innovation is the process of trying to go from Point A, to Point B, and unexpectedly landing at Point C, where true innovation happens. In the Forced Connections exercise, we bring two unrelated ideas together to try and construct an interesting and innovative new idea. For example, let's say we connect the idea of a guitar to that of a bicycle—you could have bicycle wheels made from guitar strings that play music as you ride your bike.

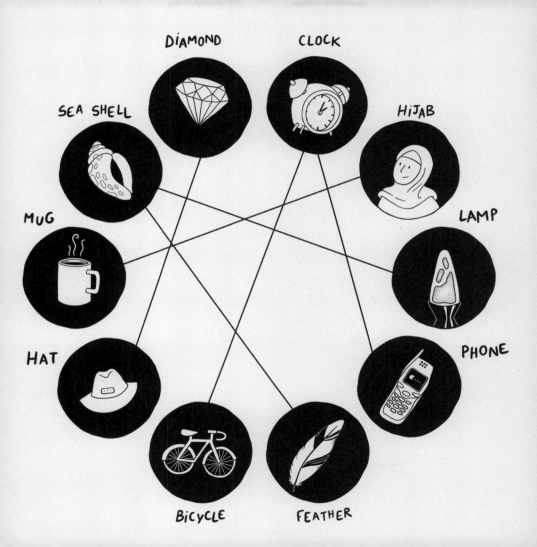

Innovation Exercises

How to Connect two images to create new, innovative ideas!

Food for Thought The more random topics that you can connect and create interesting ideas out of, the more responsive and quicker you will be to coming up with great ideas. The ideas don't need to be realistic; let creativity and imagination take the front seat.

2

Finish My Story

The idea behind the Finish My Story exercise is to show the power of collaboration. Partner up with another individual and start to tell them a random story. When it comes to creativity, you can often accomplish more with two minds than with one!

How to Set a timer to go off in intervals of every ten or fifteen seconds. Every time your timer alerts you, the other person jumps in and throws a random, off-topic word at you. You need to take that word and twist your story to fit the context of the new word. Continue for up to two minutes.

Once you are finished, you will see that your story has taken some serious twists from where you would have taken it if you had told the entire story by yourself!

If you don't have a partner to do this exercise with, you can achieve the same results using story cubes—a set of dice with different pictures on each side. Line the cubes up randomly, then come up with a story based off the pictures on each die. Start the process with, "Once upon a time . . . " and link the pictures together to form a complete story.

Food for Thought Don't think too much about what you're going to say. Continue the story in whatever way feels natural to you, adding your own flair into the narrative. Don't put any pressure on yourself, just have fun!

205

The Innovator's Handbook

3

Post-It Note Challenge

The Post-It Note Challenge is all about increasing pressure and getting the best out of your creative brain based on gut feelings and quick reactions. This is a great way to break the ice and warm up before a brainstorming session!

How to To get started, choose a subject that you want to focus on to develop ideas. For example, let's say we want to design the next stylish electric car.

With a stack of Post-It Notes and a black marker, identify a theme for your electric car. Let's assume that your first idea is "Retro Electric Car." Set your timer for sixty seconds and begin sketching what this new retro electric car may look like.

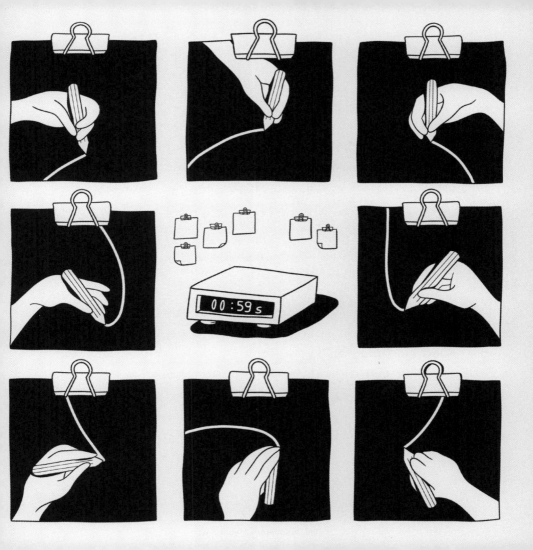

Once the time is up, everyone puts their markers down. Repeat the process again for thirty seconds, then fifteen, then ten, then five. The less time you have to think and react, the more pressure there is to come up with a quick idea. With less time to overthink things, you will discover that your initial idea was more often than not right!

Once you have finished the process several times, start sticking the Post-Its onto the wall and choose your favorite ideas—this will build a strong base for your next groundbreaking product.

Food for Thought The purpose of these innovative exercises is to get you thinking in ways that you are not used to, rather than giving you the magical recipe for coming up with innovative ideas. As always, have fun—and don't be surprised when you hit the innovation jackpot!

Innovation Exercises

4

Reverse Assumptions

Reverse Assumptions is a great tool to push yourself outside of your comfort zone and look at things differently. Choose a topic and create a list of assumptions we have about it. Then flip the assumption to the opposite.

How to Let's assume that we're designing a new bicycle. Once we have collected all our common assumptions about bicycles, we will list them, then flip (or reverse) them, giving us a fresh new perspective to look at the topic.

The Innovator's Handbook

Let's look at an example:

ASSUMPTION	FLIPPED ASSUMPTION
Bicycles have 2 wheels	Bicycles **don't** have 2 wheels
Bicycles have seats	Bicycles **don't** have seats
Bicycles have pedals	Bicycles **don't** have pedals

Food for Thought There is no magic number of solutions you should come up with—the goal is to just have fun with the process! Once you reverse your assumptions and start to brainstorm, the next step is to build on your ideas, refine them, and take them to new heights. Don't be afraid to scrap the ideas you don't like and research the strongest ones further. You set the rules. As long as you're thinking outside the box, you're good!

5

Forty Ideas in Fifteen Minutes

Forty Ideas in fifteen Minutes gets your creative juices going to the extreme. It helps you to generate many ideas about a topic in a short timeframe. With forty Ideas in fifteen Minutes, you can enjoy the results that come when you force innovation within a sprint.

How to Starting this one is simple! Take your selected idea, product, or concept and set a timer for fifteen minutes. Hit start and note down as many ideas as possible that come to mind about how to innovate that product.

Keep going, ignoring everything else, until the timer goes off. Once you are done, reflect on your ideas to see if anything jumps off the page.

Food for Thought This is a great practice that allows you to creatively design and dream without limitations. Don't judge any of your ideas, just jot them down and move on to the next thought that comes to mind. You never know what you may discover when you have fun in fifteen minutes!

6

The Future is Here

Here is another fun and engaging exercise that will help you innovate. The Future is Here encourages innovators to dream up their ideal future and develop the innovative products and concepts that will shape that future!

How To Choose a topic or product that you wish to innovate, then spend time imagining what it may look like one hundred years from now. By pushing the limit on our concept of the present, we can better imagine innovation without the present constraints.

When you develop and design products that could come on the market in one or two years, you may find that the current industry trends and cultural traits place guardrails around your concepts. The Future Is Here exercise frees you from those limitations and opens the door to untold possibilities.

Food for Thought Want to boost your creativity? Look at how things have changed a specific product or idea in the past decade or one hundred years through innovation.

The Innovator's Handbook

7

Group Sketching

This exercise explores the power of collaboration. As a group, you will decide upon a particular topic, such as a car. You will each craft your own unique vision for a car, share it with one another, and find inspiration from each other's ideas. This activity demonstrates how impactful innovation can stem from collaboration when we realize the value of others' ideas.

How to Everyone starts by writing their name on a piece of paper then starts sketching their vision. Set a timer for a certain amount of time and hand your sketch to the person next to you once the time is up.

Keep it up until your original paper comes back to you. You won't even notice it's yours, and that's okay! This exercise shows the power of collaboration and how other people's visions can influence yours, taking you on new wavelengths that you would not have thought of by yourself.

Food for Thought Keep an open mind to the contributions of those in your group. Fully explore their ideas before dismissing them. Just because something may not seem helpful at first glance doesn't mean there isn't something that can be tweaked to make it truly innovative.

The Innovator's Handbook

8

What would Brand X Do

In the What Would Brand X Do exercise, we look at how a famous person or fictional character would solve a problem with their own unique brand of innovation.

How To Take a problem or issue and imagine together how a famous person or character would solve it using their skills and outlook. For example, imagine the following ideas:

How would Steve Jobs build and market a new electric car?
How would Superman innovate the way we receive food in the future?
How would you expect the Dalai Lama to innovate banking?

Innovation Exercises

The goal is to use these unique brainstorming opportunities to "get into the head" of famous innovators and thought leaders to see how common products or ideas can be changed or improved upon to revolutionize an industry. You may be surprised by the unique solutions you come up with!

Food for Thought Combine unrelated concepts for a creativity boost. The more unrelated the person or character you choose and the subject matter, the more unexpected ideas you will have.

Great innovation only happens when people aren't afraid to do things differently.

Georg Cantor

10. WHAT WILL YOU INNOVATE NEXT?

Here is my question for you:
What will you innovate next?

My hope in writing this book is that you find both the tools and the inspiration you need to embark on your innovation journey. If you cannot put your finger on the pulse of change, and you instead stay static, you will never go from good to unforgettable. Your ideas will never rise above the competition, and the unique, irreplaceable quality you bring to the marketplace will never shine as it deserves to.

If you take one thing away from this experience, let it be this: Don't ever hold yourself and your creativity back. Your passion for what you're doing has brought you to where you are now. Tap into that passion and let it drive you to new heights. Never shun a new idea without thoroughly exploring it first. Never let your self-judgment slow your progress. The principles in this book have served me well in my time working with industry leaders, and I know they will serve you just as well.

Here's a final thought I will leave you with as you take your next steps into innovation: Never work under the assumption that your current level of creativity is where it ends. That mindset is the very thing that can keep you from accomplishing everything that you are capable of, so never stop striving.

With all that said, don't stress, and don't feel overwhelmed. Sometimes all you need to solve a creative problem is to take a break and shift your focus elsewhere, or just take a walk and relax your mind.

You have started something great, and you will achieve even greater heights from here on out. Envision that future and make it a reality. Show the world your unique perspective, and let innovation be the lifeblood that drives everything you do.

ACKNOWLEDGEMENTS

A huge thank you to my wife, Fatema, who gave me nothing but her full support and patience while I put this book together. She was part of every step of the journey as this book took shape and evolved.

A huge thanks to my wonderful parents for giving me all the support and confidence I've needed since my eyes opened to this world. You never fell short in pushing and supporting me to get to the next level. And a huge thank you to my three-year-old princess, Zahraa, who reminds me how blessed I am every day.

Thank you to my wonderful team of editors, Gregory Newton Brown, Brad Bartlett, and Isabelle Russell, for working with me to take this book to the finish line. Thank you to the amazingly talented book designers from Mano A Mano Club for their incredible work bringing this book to life as a gorgeous physical object. Thank you to Mélissa Menu for her wonderful illustrations and art throughout the book. And a special thank you to Abdelrahman Hajj for the remarkable cover art and art direction on illustrations. Finally, thanks to Liam Farrell for his creative direction, help, and support on the final details of the book. I'm so fortunate to work with such a talented team of creatives.

Thanks to my good and extremely talented friend Andrew Turner, who I learned a lot from while I was at Adidas. His help and support in exchanging ideas while writing this book was essential. I owe you.

Finally, and in no order, thanks to the wonderful friends and colleagues who always shared their ideas, thoughts, and critiques of the book as it kept evolving: Hashim Albahbahani, Jason Mayden, Leon Imas, Sam Saraf, Ahmed Alsaleh, Amod Munga, Tobie Hatfield, Tim Antoniuk, Arturo Tedeschi, Lucien Ng, Philip Stankard, Ehsan Noursalehi, Patrick Schiavone, Hector Silva, Pattrick Chew, Spencer Nugent, Reid Schlegel, Hesham Al-Sabea, Ahmed Albastaki, Marin Myftiu, Dmitry Gerais, Carl Arnese, Andrea Burnett, Claire Chao, Angela Terry, Jesse Rademacher, Daniela Paredes, Sébastien Deguy, Jeremiah Baker, Derek Sivers, Isa Alzeera, Sreejith Cheeyanjeri, Cleo Kim, James Bisset, Alexander Taylor, and Raphael Kwok.

My hope is that this this book is a starting point, not an end, to your creative journey. I feel privileged to have been able to join you on your path.

If you've made it this far, feel free to reach out and say hello: hello@mossawistudios.com. I would love to hear your thoughts and what makes you a better innovator.

You can also join The Innovator's mailing list for regular doses of innovation stories, exercises, and creative insights here:
www.mossawistudios.com/newsletter